HA
ANI
AND CRYSTAL
MAKES THREE

Written by
Steffi Gardner

Copyright © Stefanja Gardener 2023

HARRY AND ME AND CRYSTAL MAKES THREE

All rights reserved.

ISBN 978-1-914485-15-2

All rights reserved.
The right of Stefanja Gardener to be identified as the author of this work has been asserted in accordance with the Copyright, Designs and Patents Act 1988.
No part of this publication may be reproduced, stored in a retrieval system, or transmitted, in any form or by any means, electronic, mechanical, photocopying, recording or otherwise, nor translated into a machine language, without the written permission of the publisher.
This is a work of fiction. Names, characters, places and incidents are the product of the author's imagination or are used fictitiously. Any resemblance to actual persons, living or dead, events or locales is entirely coincidental.
Condition of sale. This book is sold subject to the condition that it shall not, by way of trade or otherwise, be lent, re-sold, hired out or otherwise circulated in any form of binding or cover other than that in which it is published and without a similar condition including this condition being imposed on the subsequent purchaser.

Published in 2023 by Design Marque.

Copyright © October 2023, the author, Steffi Gardner,
as named on the book cover.

The author, Steffi Gardner, has asserted her moral right under the Copyright, Designs and Patents Act, 1988 to be identified as the author of this work.

All rights reserved.
No part of this publication may be reproduced, copied, stored in a retrieval system, or transmitted, in any form or by any means, without the prior written consent of the copyright holder nor be otherwise circulated in any form of binding or cover other than that in which it is published and without a similar condition being imposed on the subsequent purchaser.

A CIP catalogue record for this title is available from the British Library.

Steffi Gardner

Also by Steffi Gardner:
For Love of Harry
Life with Harry
Charlie to the Rescue
Charlie's Quest

Cover designed by Steffi Gardner and Design Marque

HARRY
AND ME
AND CRYSTAL
MAKES THREE

Steffi Gardner

CHAPTERS

Chapter 1 7

Chapter 2 11

Chapter 3 15

Chapter 4 17

Chapter 5 23

Chapter 6 29

Chapter 7 35

Chapter 8 39

Chapter 9 43

Chapter 10 45

Chapter 11 47

Chapter 12 51

Chapter 13 53

Chapter 14 55

Chapter 15 57

Chapter 16 59

CHAPTER ONE

Hi, I'm Olly. I'm a two-year-old Miniature Schnauzer, some say with attitude. By the way, I'm named after someone special. Guess who?

I gather I am lucky to be here, because I understand my birth was unexpected. In fact, it came as a complete surprise. Apparently, my birth mum had already had puppies earlier in the year and they could be registered. However, because I was not planned, I couldn't be. So now you know.

I have three brothers and one sister. They went to new homes fairly quickly but for some reason no-one wanted me. That's what my birth mum said but I knew she was wrong. The right person for me just hadn't turned up yet!

Turns out my birth dad was a wuss, and I think was 'losing it.' Tell you why. He barked a lot and at times stared into space. According to the tv this is not normal behaviour.

Three months went by, and I was just starting to wonder if I had got it wrong. Was my special person coming? Soon I was told. Soon. Now, before you ask me I have no idea where those words came from, but they felt right, and I relaxed. I had to trust. All of a sudden, the doorbell rang. I heard it from outside. I had been playing with my favourite toy, when I was rudely picked up and brought into the house. There were strangers. A man, a woman and two dogs. I gave them a quick look then carried on playing.

The people looked at me and one of the dogs growled. So what? I wasn't scared. The white dog was quiet. He'll be no trouble I thought. 'Their names are Crystal and Harry' I heard the woman say. Harry looked a little like me. He smelled a little like me too though he was a different colour. I wasn't sure what Crystal was. Turns out she is a Cocker Spaniel, a Blue Roan. That means she is a black dog but has a layer of black and white added plus a layer of white. She is bigger than me! At the time I first met them, she was about twelve, and Harry seven or eight. Apparently, he's a rescue.

He looked sad. I found out why much later. He had lost his bestie, a Golden Retriever called Tally. He loved her to bits. She had mothered him from the word go, when mum had adopted him. Crystal told me that she remembered that day very well, and the time that followed. She told me he was so traumatized he could not walk properly or think. She still feels that it hurts him to think about that time. Why? She says that when he seems lost in thought he smells slightly different.

When my new mum brought him home Harry remembers being so terrified, he was going to be hurt again, his mind shut down. So, it was always my new mum/guardian who had most to do with Tally and Harry, and, as it turned out later, me.

During one of our talks, which came months after my arrival, when Harry had relaxed with me, I asked him what he thought of Crystal. He hesitated then told me that he was still slightly nervous of her and makes sure he is nowhere near her especially at mealtimes. Why? 'She has to be fed separately as she is food aggressive' he said. Know how he feels as I wouldn't want anyone to pinch my food. Fortunately, I was sure there'd be loads to go round, and as I'm quite placid, well mostly, I never have a problem with food. But I do steer clear of Crystal sometimes, as if there is even one scrap of food about and she thinks I want it she goes for me.

Can't say I particularly like Crystal even now, but on the whole, I suppose we get on reasonably well, though if she has something and she thinks I want it she growls. She does what the books and tv say 'guards it' and will only let mum or dad take it away. Now, would you say this is nice behaviour? It isn't, is it? But honestly, she does not like to share!

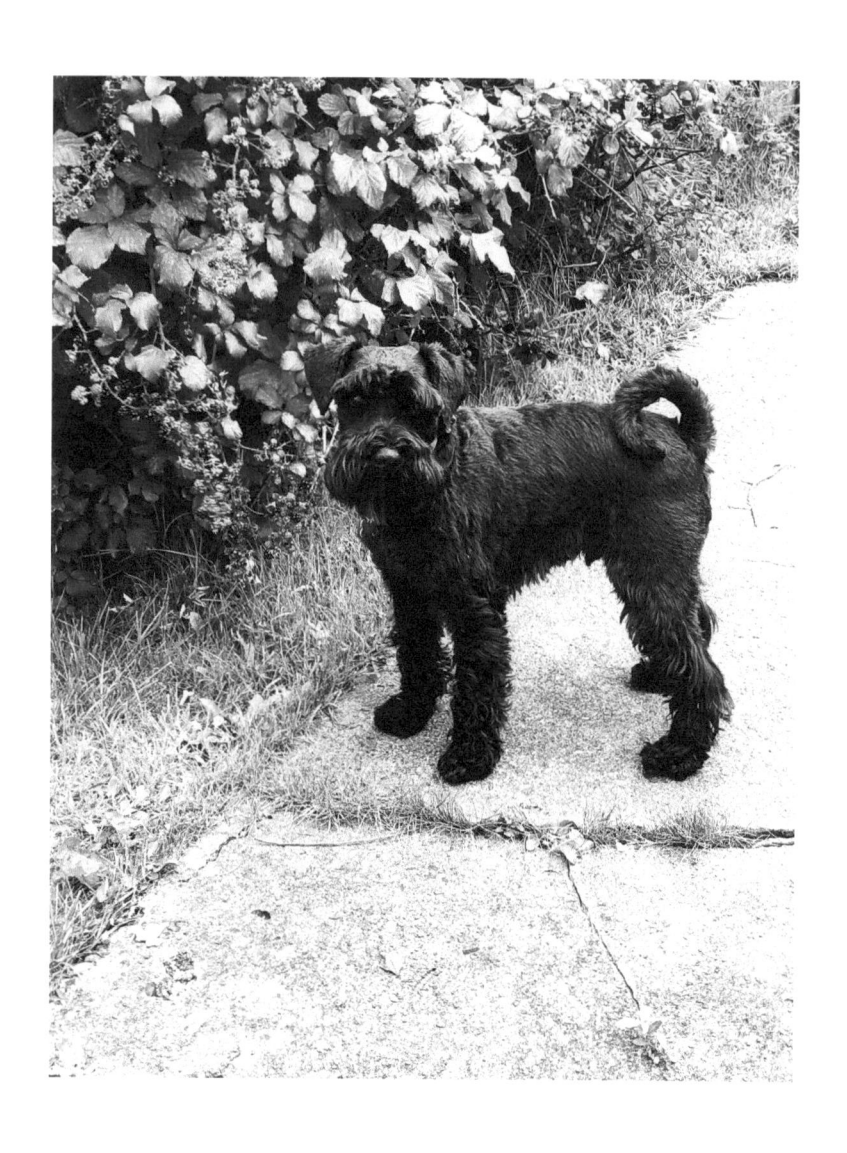

CHAPTER TWO

Now, back to my story and what happened on that day – the day I met my new mum and dad. As I said, I could see Harry was very quiet. He didn't look around, just sat with his head down. It didn't really matter though as I had loads of energy and was quite happy to play games with my tug toy and the lady I hoped would be my new mum/guardian.

She felt right to me and no I can't explain it. It is just something you feel or know! I don't think my new dad was struck on me though as he didn't say much, except that Crystal had growled at me. Mum explained that sometimes that happened, and it would have been better had we all been able to go outside and meet up initially. Dad didn't look convinced. However, I knew that if I made a fuss of mum that'd probably do the trick. After all, who can resist a cute puppy, and although I say it myself, I was and still am cute!

Note to all of you who are reading this story, remind your dog always to remain cute, no matter what it takes. A roll on your back guys, if you feel up to it. Not a roll through fear though, but one when you are relaxed and happy to have your tum stroked. Then sit staring with puppy eyes and look pitiful. These things do work! So, if there's a problem you get away with it – mostly!

However, at the breeder's house before mum bought me there was quite a discussion. She thought I had these things called papers and was unhappy there weren't, and she hadn't been told in advance. The person selling me explained about the unplanned mating thing and that I wasn't registered.

Oh no, please don't leave me mum I thought. I concentrated and sent out these vibe things. Positive thinking. It's a gift I have. Fortunately, although she was quiet, she still seemed to want me though and didn't let the papers thing put her off. Dad didn't look happy. She was given something called a pedigree certificate which told her who my parents, grandparents etc. were, but guess what, she has lost it! Typical, she is a bit scatty to say the least. She was telling a friend that she knew that she put it somewhere. She just can't find it!

It was a long ride to my new home, but mum asked dad to drive as she wanted to nurse me all the way, so her scent would be imprinted on me. Not quite sure what that meant except to say I breathed in her smell and felt safe. She told me of all the lovely places we would be going to for walks and that there was a beach nearby. Wasn't sure what that was or sand, but it sounded nice. I found out it is! The sound of the car was soothing, so I curled up and went to sleep. Crystal and Harry did the same.

My new home had its own smells and from the beginning I loved these. Could do with a bigger garden though. However, you can't have everything, and as we are near a beach, woods and the coastal path it's okay.

'Training is up to you as you wanted him' dad said to mum. Training? What training? Come on, first things first! What I wanted to know was where was the food? Mum put me down in the garden with Harry and Crystal and called 'wee wee, wee wee'. What did that mean? I saw Harry and Crystal do something. I sniffed. It smelled ok, so I decided to do the same. Mum praised me saying what a clever boy I was.

Back in the house we were all in the kitchen. I could smell food, but where was it? I was hungry. Mum was standing by the sink with three bowls. Oh, at last! In the other house I was always fed in my crate and slept there too. Would it be the same here? Crystal, who was barking her head off for food was fed on her own. Harry and I ate ours peacefully. Then a call from mum to go outside again. Why? I had already been. Mum kept on saying 'wee wee', but I took no notice. I was too busy exploring. We all came back inside, and Harry curled up in his bed with Crystal in another. She growled. Harry just lay there looking at me.

Mum turned round to put the kettle on to make tea, so she didn't see me do a wee, but dad did. Out I went again. This time with dad as mum had to clean the floor. I didn't want to do anything of course, so I decided to do the necessary inside when I was ready. That included leaving some little parcels on the kitchen floor which mum cleaned up. Once she caught me in the act and put me outside telling me what a good boy I was when I obliged and making silly noises. The trouble was by then I had lost interest and didn't want to go.

Now, before you ask me, no I don't know how long it was before I stopped leaving little presents. I do know that mum kept asking dad to make sure all the inside doors were closed, including the bathroom. She did get a bit cross once when she asked him to keep an eye on me and he forgot because he was reading a book.

Although it did take dad a while, and he wouldn't tell you, he loves me now, feeds me from time to time and takes me on walks with Crystal. He doesn't clear up if I am sick though. He did agree eventually that I was good for Harry who is still very nervous. I think he realizes too just how special I am, especially when it looked as though someone was trying to take me!

Eventually, I did learn to go outside and since then I haven't looked back, though I still go when it suits me. I like to see mum standing in the rain at night in her coat saying 'wee wee'. She looks so funny! Now, don't get me wrong. I love my new guardians, though mum has more to do with me, as she prepares most of the food and stands outside with us when it is raining.

CHAPTER THREE

TRAINING!

Like you I had to go to class to learn things, though some took 'longer than normal', whatever that means! For instance, the lady running the class couldn't understand why I would not lie down on command. All the others obeyed and quickly too, but I am not like the others.

I'm not sure why I wouldn't lie down. I just didn't want to. Was it the way she told me to do it, rather than coaxed me, or was it because I had a mind of my own. The lady even tried using treats and holding them under a small pole raised slightly off the ground. Gather I was supposed to lie down to reach them. However, although I put my front paws down my bottom remained up. The lady said she didn't know what to do as she had never come across a dog like me! 'Let's leave it for a while. Practise at home. Perhaps he is too dominant.' Me!!

On the way home I thought about things. When we had to practise a recall, I was the only one who came bounding back each time straight to mum. The others took their time. Some stopped and sniffed. Others ran past. Not me. I was straight there. Every time! If I didn't lie down at home, why should I do it in a strange place with a lot of other dogs around? If you were a dog would you do it?

Now, before you ask me, no I am not stubborn. I agree I did make a lot of noise and sometimes would have water squirted at me, but all I wanted to do was to go and say hello to all the other dogs there. Apparently, after the first time a general meet and greet was not allowed. Eventually, at home mum persuaded me to lie down. Gosh what a fuss she made of me. I had watched Crystal lie down and saw she was getting treats so decided to copy her. Now I lie down when asked in the house, in the garden, and at times on the beach. This depends on who's there of course!

Harry doesn't lie down as he is too nervous. Mum tried but, in the end, it upset him so much she stopped. He said, 'when he tried it his head hurt.' I wonder what was done to him before he came to mum.

Do you know he couldn't even sit when in the garden or out on walks, even if there was a treat involved. He told me that his mind went blank. He must be getting better though as now he does. He will still shrink away from things he said but I think as a rescue from a puppy farm he hadn't had a good life. Even though he is safe now and on the whole, I think happy, especially since I came, there are times when he appears lost. He sits and stares into space. Not like my old dad, but as though he is trying to process things. Times like that he smells slightly different as though some changes are going on. Heard mum telling dad recently that when people are worried, or anxious or traumatized their bodies can give out different chemical smells. Must be the same for dogs I reckon.

CHAPTER FOUR

One day when we were all in the garden, I asked Harry about himself. He said all he knew was that he had come a very long way in a van to a place where there were more people and a lot of dogs. He didn't know how long he had been there, and it was scary, though the people this time were kind and didn't hurt him. Imagine being deliberately hurt. How can anyone do that to us?

Anyway, he had been in this new place and was waiting with other dogs to see the vet man to have some sort of operation, when mum came to see him. He didn't remember much about her the first time except that she smelled ok, and he felt safe when she held him.

At first, Harry was worried about telling me things but in the end, he did agree to talk about some of the things he remembered. When he arrived at this other place, he said that he felt so terrified that he stayed curled up near the back of his pen, hoping no one would see him. However, the lady at the rescue centre came to get him for the operation. All he remembers was feeling terrified and squashing himself against the sides of the pen. He vaguely recalled the lady at the centre telling mum that he wouldn't look at anyone and was petrified of being picked up. 'He goes rigid' she said. I can't imagine what that would have been like and hope I never will.

Thinking about it I feel Harry is incredibly brave to have survived that and begun to trust, even though it has taken him a very very long time. Years! He seems much better now and will sometimes play with me outside. He will run towards me or alongside me for a few minutes. This is fun though it is never for long. I think maybe I get a little rough at times or maybe too excited as mum has to tell me off.

Now, this is really strange but truly I haven't made it up. One day when Harry and I were talking, and Crystal just happened to be listening, he said that mum had a telephone call from a friend of hers who lived far away, in a place called France. Mum was talking on the 'phone and Harry said that he stared at her as if he was trying to remember. He reckoned some of the words sounded familiar, but the memory was so long ago he couldn't be sure.

It got me thinking. We all have these things called microchips which are inserted in the back of our necks when we are small. I think they are there so that if we are lost or stolen a vet can scan the chip and it tells him (well it might depend on whether someone has illegally removed the chip or not) who our guardians are and where they live.

Bet you don't know this, but I heard mum talking to the vet when he scanned my chip. Some vets think chips are inserted into the larger and slower maturing breeds far too soon. So, when muscle and fat build up the chip can't always be located. What do you reckon about that? More importantly, Crystal and I wondered where Harry had been born and how he ended up first of all on a puppy farm and then at one rescue centre, then another. Was he in fact an illegal immigrant? We will never know, but mum did manage to find out that his microchip had been inserted in Scotland. However, as I heard her say to her best friend in Bristol it didn't mean that he had been born there!

Now to the important stuff. Do you ever know something without being told? I do. It's like I have been here before! And it didn't take me long to realise that although I knew I was loved I was there also to try and help Harry – bet you guessed that!

I feel very proud about this. Don't ever tell him I told you, but do you know he was still so terrified about coming through doors he would stand out even in the rain and mum had to carry him in and dry him off with a towel. Now he follows me most of the time, provided mum is not standing by the outside door.

Something else, and this is really important, as it makes my mum happy, I heard her say recently that Harry appears to have found his voice. Not exactly sure what this means. Could it be that he barks more and will now come to her when it is near teatime to say, 'it's time?'

Heard her tell dad that she read somewhere that it means he now feels part of his pack. Suppose that makes sense! I've seen him occasionally put his paws on the settee and look at her, and he wags his tail a lot more. Well, I think those things must be good, don't you? Well, apart from the barking. That's all Crystal's fault. He's picked that up from her!

As to fears I don't have any as such. Well not that I know of. I launch myself at mum when she is sitting. I also tear up what I can find, and make off with them, including what I can pinch from the laundry basket. Socks are my favourite because you can play with them; shake them as if they're a rat. Remember we were originally bred to be rat catchers, so it's in the genes. I then toss the socks in the air and start again. I don't usually bring them back and often leave them in the garden, especially if it is raining. I do not like carrying wet socks.

It's good exercise' dad says as mum searches for what I have left outside Wonder why he doesn't say that when it's his socks, or underpants, etc? Personally, I don't see the difference, whether it's mum's or dad's. You may well ask what Crystal's doing all this time. Grabs toys and walks around with them in her mouth. She will even chase and grab those that are thrown for me. Girls!

In case you are wondering how much worse things can be, training wise, let me tell you I am quite obedient now. I can run on the beach and usually come back to mum when she calls me. I say usually because at times I really want to go and say hello. Sometimes, on my way back, I head off in the wrong direction, and then she needs to call my name and wave her arms. She tried using a whistle to get my attention, but Harry doesn't like it and cowers, so she gave up on that.

When dad takes me for a walk, I have to wear something called a head collar. I am pretty strong and nothing else slows me down. I don't mind really as it doesn't hurt at all. It is nice and soft, and I suppose it does make me listen more, especially if there's a dog I'm interested in or want to greet. Off the lead on the beach, I wear a harness. Why? Well, it is attached to a long line to stop me running after or up to other dogs. Some don't like this, and mum wants me to listen to her and come back when she calls. It is all part of my training.

Did you know that we dogs go through several stages of learning or development? At the moment I am said to be in the terrible teenage years. This is when I want to do my own thing and not listen. Are you there yet or are you really good and always paying attention? Sometimes if I am very quick, I manage to get away before mum gets the end of the lead sorted out. This is definitely a fun game, but she is getting better now.

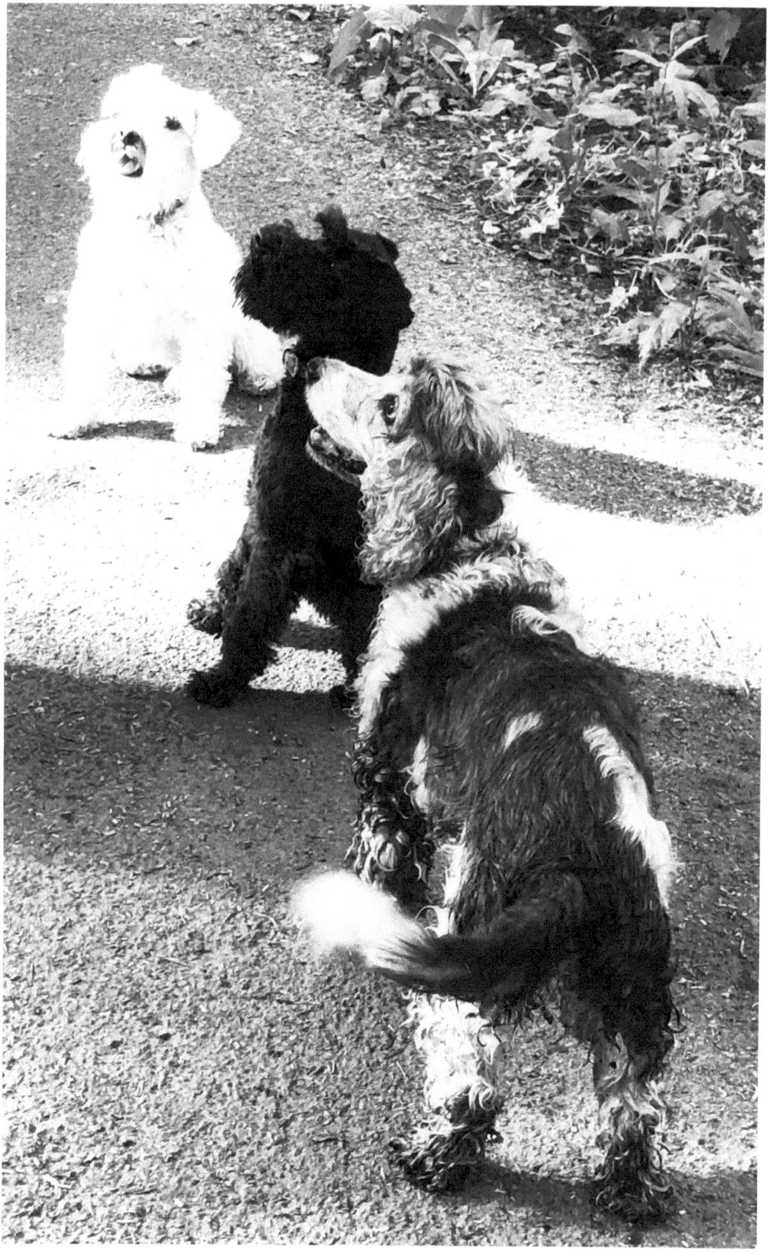

CHAPTER FIVE

I love walks and being off the lead, and we often go in the car to different places. One is these is a park. There are woods to explore, and loads of hidden places where the smells are great. When there are no dogs about Harry is let off the lead. He does settle down if mum and I are there, but always yells a lot first. Sometimes dad and Crystal come with us.

They prefer longer walks though. Having said that, all Crystal seems interested in when with us is her ball, unless there is water. Then she is deaf to all entreaties. That means 'yells', to come out. Selective deafness mums calls it, but dad disagrees.

At the moment I am lying on the settee in the lounge. Harry and Crystal are in their beds in the kitchen. We've all had tea: mince, biscuits, vegetables, and apple, plus! Not bad for a Tuesday!! Some cooked chicken is my all time favourite, and fortunately I don't have problems with that: but mince comes second. Turkey mince, which we don't get very often, is a third. We also get the odd treat or two – small pieces of home made liver cake, and some bone broth – now you're talking!

Anyway, lying here, I have time to think about what I want to share with you next. There are two things. Home Boarding, and mum's car. Let's start with home boarding. Usually when mum and dad go away at the same time we go to kennels . However, mum heard of a lady who doesn't live far away who takes in dogs when their guardians are away.   She rang up and the lady said to come and look and bring the dogs initially for a 'meet and greet' with her own dogs.

Now, as you know, I know all about 'meet and greet.' Dad said that it sounded ideal, 'With your leg as it is it will be much easier and only a 20 minute drive away' he said. So mum put us in the car and drove to see the lady. We turned in through the open gate on to a gravel drive. As mum drove up the lady came out of the house. Bring them out she said. Mine are in the garden. This was surrounded by fencing. Mum lifted us out of the car. We were all on leads. I was rarin' to go and was pulling because I wanted to explore. Mum was limping a little. Harry hung back a little. Where was Crystal? Dad had gone to see an old friend, a walker, who lived in the north of England.

'I can see he is strong' the lady said. I looked round. New place, new smells. I christened a car wheel (not mum's I hasten to add) just so everyone knew I was there, and also the fence. Harry did nothing, though he looked uneasy. Her dogs were in the garden and we all 'introduced' ourselves. I don't know what breed her dogs were but they were smaller than us. Her male dogs did a wee, and I followed suit. 'So far so good' the lady said. 'I don't think there will be any problems.' I could sense mum wasn't sure. 'Harry is a rescue she said, and nervous.' The lady said something like that was fine.   'Bring them back another time for half a day so they get used to being here. While she was there mum asked loads of questions, like where would we be sleeping , exercised, walked and what outside freedom we would have during the day. When dad rang that evening he asked mum what she thought. 'I'm not sure' was her reply.   'Something doesn't feel right. Can't put my finger on it but....'

Anyway later in the week she took us back. The lady showed us round telling mum that we had freedom to go in and out of the house and garden etc. There was a plastic curtain hanging near the back door and all the dogs had to go through that. It was arranged that mum would come collect us at 5pm. Later that evening (and we were all back at home by then) Mum told her friend she had been back in the house for about half an hour when the lady rang. 'Please come and collect them' she said. 'Olly has cocked his leg in the lounge; my dogs are on the settee barking at yours , and Harry has done a mess and won't stop barking. It is doing my head in.' Apparently, mum said she was very sorry and collected us straight away. The lady was pleased to see the back of us and we were pleased. I was delighted , Harry even more so, to be going home with mum. As soon as he saw mum he stopped barking and couldn't wait to get back in the car. Neither of us liked the place or the lady. We much prefer Kate.

Mum was so upset about what happened she rang a doggy friend, Maureen, in Bristol. 'Well, I knew you weren't happy initially when you rang me. But honestly what did she expect?' her friend said. 'Normal behaviour when a dog comes into someone else's house where there are male and female dogs. Mind you I always brings new dogs initially into the kitchen, and also let them spend plenty of time together in the garden.' Mum said to dad that she felt much better after that. So that's the home boarding thing out of the way. We are better off with Kate, and mum feels happier too.

Now, what's next? Oh yes, mum's car. What's wrong with it, you may ask? As far as I can tell, nothing. It's mum really. She's had problems with her knee, and when she changed her last car, before the operation, she bought something called an SV, because it was higher off the ground so she didn't have to bend down to get in. Unfortunately, Crystal said that mum didn't ask the right questions at the garage, or they didn't tell her it had a sports suspension. Crystal can't remember exactly what mum told dad, but when the car goes over bumps and potholes, and there are a lot where we live, it hurts her neck. Must admit, I've never had any trouble. I'm always comfy on blankets in the back seat, but I guess mum isn't as well put together as I am. Also, I do take what Crystal says with a pinch of salt, at times at least. I think she sometimes makes things up as she wants to appear in the know. However, on this occasion!

Now, where was I? Oh yes, I remember. I gather mum is thinking of changing her car again. Unfortunately, she can't make up her mind what to have. A second hand one definitely. A 1.0TSI didn't have enough vroom. The 1.5TSI is much better but, of course, it costs more. In the end she decided it had to be the one with the larger engine and she looked at one. However, she took so long deciding it was sold. There was another but she didn't like the colour. It was two tone. That means it was two different colours. The roof was red and the rest of the car was black. Does that really matter? Anyway, she did the same thing again, spent too long deciding so that went too. 'Just make your mind up' said dad. I agree. Just go for it. It's only a car!

Well, here's the latest update. She finally bought one: thank goodness for that. I heard her tell dad and friends that although she had no choice as to colour she likes it. It felt right. It is quite comfy. We all agree on that. All she has to do now is learn to park it! She and dad were out the other day, and we were, as usual, sitting quietly in the back. After trying three or maybe four times to get it right into the square she finally realised she needs to drive further forward towards the line. Why she and dad have a problem with this none of us is sure. I ask you, what's a longer bonnet got to do with it?

'If you are not sure just get out and have a look' said dad. Had to laugh because he is no better. In fact several times he has parked half in one box and half in another. On one occasion a woman standing next to mum while she watched dad park asked if he was with her . She said it with a laugh but I could tell what she was thinking. Mum just smiled and said that it was a new car and they both had to get used to it. Good reply mum! Tell you something else. On another occasion when mum had to park, we were looking over the back seat as usual, clipped on to seat belts for safety. What did we see behind us? Another car just like mum's. Guess what, the driver was having the same problem. So, it's not just mum. What we particularly like about this car though is that the side windows are a darker shade, which means it is cooler inside for us.

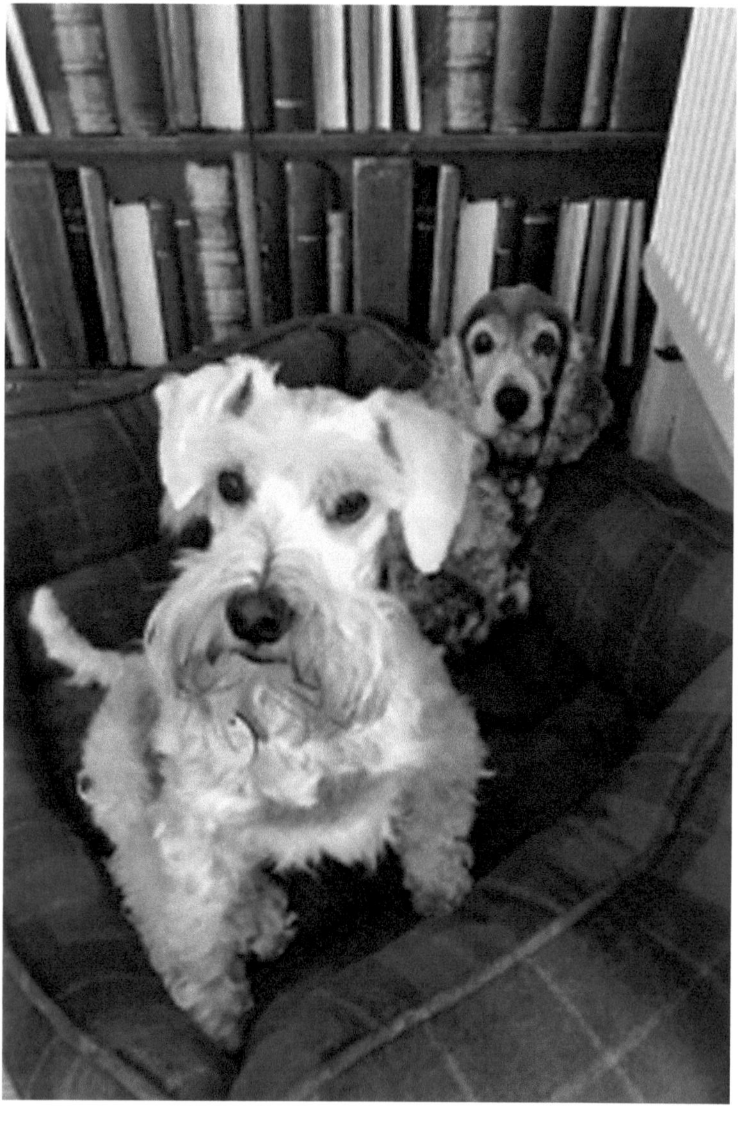

CHAPTER SIX

Now we come to this thing called a ramp. I gather it is used for dogs to get in and out of cars easily. Dad had it from a friend who was moving to a retirement village in a place called Surrey. He and his wife had bought a smaller car so didn't need it. 'It will be good to use,' said dad. 'Save you lifting the dogs in and out of the car.' He has loads of good ideas, unfortunately!

First the ramp was laid out flat in the garden and we were encouraged to walk on it. Then days later it was put on the steps into the garden. I gather we were supposed to use it. No way. It was easier to jump down the steps. 'You need to persevere,' said dad. 'It takes time!' However, a week later we were still jumping down the steps. 'You aren't doing it properly,' said dad. Didn't catch what mum said as dad wandered off. No more ramps. I think it went into the garage or mum took it to the tip. Not sure!

Mum drove us to our favourite park the other Saturday. It had been very sunny for days, so she got up early. Fortunately, the gate was open. We were the only ones there. As soon as he got out of the car Harry as usual was yelling his head off - excitement Crystal reckoned. I tuned him out and concentrated on sniffing. Crystal had wandered off somewhere again, though soon came back when she heard the magic word 'treats.' Dad said that she was getting deaf. I don't reckon she can be. Why? 'Because she hears certain things, even at a distance?

She was sulking when we drove home. We all had to sit in the back of the car. No, not on the seats but in the boot this time. Mum had put in mats so we didn't slide about, but Crystal said it wasn't good enough and we should have been in the back. Thinking about it I reckon she wanted her own space and being in the boot meant the three of us were sitting fairly closely together.

Now, you know Crystal; well, you should by now! She likes to stretch out in her 'donut' fluffy bed. She can't do that in the boot of the car. I didn't say anything. Well, you know me: tact personified! However, I reckon she was miffed because she had to share her space with us and didn't have her comfy bed there. What do you reckon? Whatever it was she didn't like it.

We stopped briefly for mum to go to the shops. Before you ask, it was cool. Mum parked in the shade and all the windows were open. We were comfortable but Crystal sat there and barked and barked and barked. Harry? Well like me, he was quiet. Good job it wasn't busy as I would have been embarrassed listening to her bark her head off for no good reason. What would people have thought of us?

Mum's been busy in the garden. She bought some mushroom compost from a gardener called Dave. He reckoned it was a good rose feed. Of course, I had to sniff it. It smelled good. It was not my fault I got to it before she watered it in. Before you ask, I did not pick any of it out of a container. It must have been the wind that blew it out of the pot! Mum told me off which was totally unfair. Must remember to carry it further next time!

I've not been very well lately, though I'm a lot better now. I must have eaten something nasty because I had a pain in my tum and all my poos were runny and bloody. 'I'm going to the vet' mum said. Just as well, as I daren't move so just sat outside on the daffodils. I was ill in the kitchen too, but mum washed me, then the floor needed cleaning. Dad had disappeared. He's not good with the mop!

Several days later I began to feel better and wanted to eat. The vet had said if I wasn't weeing, I needed to go back. Apparently, Minis are susceptible to kidney stones. She said I was young for those but as we boys have smaller bladders if there was a stone, and it was stuck I needed an operation. Fortunately, there wasn't one and I didn't.

Oh, something's happening. The box on wheels, a suitcase mum calls it, is downstairs, and she and dad are putting things in it. Now, this is interesting. Our large crate is in the hall. Crystal reckons that means we are all going somewhere. I wonder where? Will I like it? This time we were on the back seat, as our large travel crate, with rugs and bedding, towels, and suitcase etc on top was in the boot. Why do people have to take so much junk on holiday? We manage with much less! Food, water bowls, wet weather coats and leads. What more do we need?

Guess what. We went to Breconshire. Mum had to see a lady in the Tourist Office in a place called Libanus. She had to give the lady some copies of one of her books. It was a sunny day but windy, and afterwards we all started out on a walk. Unfortunately, Harry didn't like the wind and kept barking, though it felt a little like crying to me. In the end mum decided to take him back to the car.

When we got back later, she said to dad that as soon as Harry saw the car he wanted to jump in. When mum lifted him in apparently, he just curled up on the seat and went to sleep. Wonder if the wind reminded him of the time he was lost?

Crystal and I enjoyed exploring the path dad took us on. The smells were different. We didn't mind the wind one little bit, as we were too busy exploring. Had to laugh as dad's cap kept blowing off. I would have liked it better if dad had let me off the lead, but Crystal said we had to stay on leads as there were sheep about. They left us all safely in the car and went to get a cuppa.

We are now in a hotel, in a place called Crickhowell. It's lovely. There are wonderful cooking smells. Wonder what we've got for tea? Our room was ok. Plenty of room for our crate. Mum and dad have a bed to sleep in, and we have our crate with nice thick bedding. Guess who keeps turning round and round in circles, taking up far too much room! Still, we had a good walk earlier so maybe it won't be too bad. Great: teatime. That smells good. Wonder how long we are here for? Mum's going to a talk tonight – something to do with hill ponies and biodiversity and the breeding of Welsh Mountain Ponies. Dad said he would rather take us for another walk though she had bought him a ticket! They would meet up for a drink later. Before we went to sleep, we heard them nattering.

I gather the talk was quite interesting, but mum doesn't go to this place as often as she would like to hear lectures. It's too far to drive, listen to the lecture, then drive home in one day, she said. She was slightly upset though as I gather no-one came to say hello. Reckon that's mean. I always go and say hello to everyone!

However, she quite liked what was discussed though she thought that the survey thing should have been carried out by a university in Wales, as it was the Breconshire Beacons, they had studied, not somewhere in England. The Beacons now has a new name but I can't pronounce it. Mum said it is pronounced Ban-eye Bruck-ein-iog. She didn't understand why the university had applied and been given something called a grant - Crystal said that meant money, to carry out research in Wales. It didn't seem to make sense to her, but we won't go into that!

Later on, I asked Crystal why mum had wanted to hear about hill ponies. Crystal wasn't sure but wondered if she might want the information for another of Charlie's stories. She didn't seem that interested in giving me more information; just turned round and went to sleep. When I talked to Harry about this, he thought that perhaps Crystal didn't really know anything but wanted to make out she was in the know. Why doesn't that surprise me?

We've been home for ages now and although we have had walks to the beach I want to explore more. What I love about the beach is the smells, the sea, the seaweed, the rock pools, and the smells other dogs have left for me to find. Dogs are good like that you know. When I'm on my own with mum and there is plenty of sand, she throws me treats and tells me to 'search'. It is a good game. Nose down I sniff until I find whatever the treat is. My favourite is small, cooked pieces of dried liver.

You've probably realized that although I am happy to be out with the others, I prefer it when it is just the two of us - mum and me. That's our special time. The other day mum yelled 'Come on, we're going' She shook the car keys and lifted us into the car. 'This looks interesting' I thought. When the car stopped, we were in a small car park, near woods. Wow, off the lead! Harry and I whizzed off. All those lovely smells. All those paths to explore. I know there must be other dogs about as there were several cars in the car park, but it's very quiet here.

To the left of the path are sawn off tree trunks and banks and ditches. I go to explore, and Harry follows. No Crystal today. She is snoozing at home. I go to investigate the ditches and am thinking of jumping down then I hear mum's voice. 'No'. Ok mum I was only thinking about it honestly! I'm not that keen really, and I was going to come back. I turn back to the path. Woods to the right. Now that looks interesting. Harry follows me keeping quiet.

CHAPTER SEVEN

The sun is not yet shining through the trees, but I can hear the birds singing. I haven't been to this part before, and I like it. I keep exploring to the left and right of the path; there are some lovely smells. Harry joins me.

Now this looks interesting. Up ahead to the right are these strange waddling bird-like things. Ducks I learn later. As Harry and I run towards them they waddle with a quack into the water. It is a large pond. Spoilsports. I had decided before they went in the water, I was going to chase them, but when I stopped on the bank, I saw the water was deep, so I decided it wasn't worth the effort.

I also remembered that when we all walked here before Crystal had been in and out of the water. Although dad had called her to come, Crystal, being Crystal, had ignored him. She thinks if she keeps wagging her tail and looking as if she hasn't heard dad, she will be fine. We went to the end of the woods and turned back to the car park. Must tell you that I heard mum say that Crystal was not getting into her clean car.

Harry and I didn't really hear what dad said, but I did hear that mum said he could dry her with his old coat. All he had to do then was to put the coat in the wash. Fortunately, there was a rug of sorts in the boot and dad dried her off before mum said he'd better put her in with us. Dad had volunteered to walk with Crystal, to where they were going. 'She'll have dried off by then' he said.   Guess what, mum was going to have a beauty treatment. I thought that was a good idea as at her age she needs it.

However, on second thoughts that sounds a mean thing to say, and I don't have a mean bone in my body. I heard mum telling someone that about me and I gather it means that I am nice. I am, of course, but it was lovely to hear her say it. I think what I should have said was that how lovely it was that mum was having a beauty treatment as she was sure to find it relaxing!   Dad was going to wait and have a cup of tea.

As mum drove along to the treatment place, I heard dad comment that he hadn't realised it was quite so far. 'Just as well you didn't have to walk then' was mum's reply. She said it with a smile in her voice. Personally, I think it would have served Crystal right if she'd had to walk.

Then next time mum took us to the woods Harry, mum and I saw a man and woman and two big dogs. They didn't have any hair on. They were called Whippets. The man and woman and mum stopped to talk. Harry was fine with the dogs. They were a mum and daughter and very gentle. They just sniffed him, and he didn't get upset.   They sniffed me too. In fact, in true doggy fashion, we four dogs said 'hello'.   Mum took a few photos. She did ask the dogs' names, but, unfortunately, guess what, she forgot them. Hope we see them again. The couple asked about us and mum explained that Harry was a rescue. The nice man and woman knew about rescue dogs as they had an elderly one at home.

Do you know, I can always tell if people are nice because they speak in a certain way, and always have loads of treats in their pockets. What else? Well, they are kind and patient. They make slow movements with their hands, bend down to talk to us and let us come to them. What was lovely was that Harry went up to the man and allowed him to pat him. Wow mum, wasn't that amazing? He did not back away. I could tell mum was pleased as her voice altered and she was smiling. They were definitely a nice couple. The dogs shot off. 'After squirrels', the man said. 'They never catch them, but Whippets are sight hounds, and they like to chase things.'

Think I've told you that we do this seek and search thing in the garden. Mum keeps us inside while she goes out and scatters small treats, so we have to use our brains and noses to find them. Although we are used to this now and always know when it is coming it is still exciting. Harry certainly thinks so as he yells his head off. Crystal is always first at the door barking and scrabbling, followed by Harry and then me.

When mum opens the door, we are there, yelling with delight – well Harry is. We dash down the steps into the garden. Crystal has a habit, a bad one I might add, of hoovering everything up as quickly as possible. Then yells to come back in.

I was on the beach with mum the other day, straining to be let off the lead: new friends to meet. They all smelled fine, and we got on well, dashing back and forwards across the beach. Then the others splashed through the sea to get to the other side. However, I am not keen on getting my feet wet, so looked round for mum then came back. She was delighted, telling me how good I was. So, I thought I'd better keep quiet about my reason for returning so promptly.

It's been very hot lately, and we are starting to get used to waiting by the door now, bright and early, while it is cool, for

Mum to take us somewhere in the car. I wonder, where it will be today? The park, the woods, or the woodland walk? Come on mum, where are you? Time to get up. It's 6.30 am and we are rarin' to go. I can understand why she has to make sure she has the scented 'poo bags', and treats, but why on earth does she have to have a drink before leaving? She can make one when she gets back. At last, we are in the car. Not long now!

That was lovely. It started to rain slightly just after we started our walk, but the leaves on the trees sheltered mum from most of it. The rain on the leaves sounded like pitter patter, pitter patter. Think you know what that sounds like. Do you find that reassuring? I know I do. Funnily enough it doesn't seem to bother Harry, which is good.

Have you ever been out early in the morning? It is so peaceful. You can hear the birds sing and if you are lucky see them on the path. Though as soon as they see or hear us, they fly away or on to the nearest branch for safety. I love the smell of the earth after it has rained. It all smells so different. Harry doesn't sniff much though he is getting better at exploring. Generally, he follows me though unlike me he doesn't like to run up the banks, preferring to stay near the path. Having said that I found a path I had not explored before, and he did come after me for a while before turning back to find mum.

CHAPTER EIGHT

Something exciting is happening. I can smell it and I hear mum talking about it on the phone. She and dad are off on holiday. No, we can't go with them because they are going to this place called France for something called a wedding.

Think it must be nice because mum has bought a new dress and has been asking all her friends whether it suits her. Why she has to ask so many people I don't know. She must like it after all, as she bought it. However, the next big thing are shoes. She saw these lovely ones, the same shade as the main colour on her dress. So, she ordered them. Unfortunately, when they came, they were a little too high and too tight. You've probably guessed: mum has problems with her feet. Ssh, don't tell her I told you.

Well, she tried to return them, but couldn't. Why? because the tiny writing on the site said that they were made to measure and therefore could not be returned. Listening to her talking to dad I did agree. They were a standard size, and you had to read the advertisement very closely indeed to see what it said about being made to measure. She won't be shopping with them again.

By now mum was getting a little worried. I could hear it in her voice. Your voices tell us a lot about you, so be careful! She needed smart shoes but couldn't wear anything with much of a heel. Finally, just when I was fed up hearing about her shoes a friend found a solution. Buy those toe cap things that fit over your toes. That way you can walk in the shoes and not damage your toes. Brilliant.

It seemed to work in the house. So, mum put them away safely with the shoes, and handbag etc. Now, guess what happened? Oh, I see you too have a mum like mine. Several days before they were due to go away, someone couldn't find the toe thingies. The shoes, bag, etc were all there. Again, I heard her on the phone calling a friend. You'll never guess what they came up with? Plasters. That's right, sticking plasters. 'If you fix one on each toe your toes won't be rubbed' said her friend Lynn.

The day before they went mum took the three of us to the kennels. When Crystal realised where we were she tried to jump back in the car. Honestly, that dog is no fun at times. Why she can't explore like me I do not know. Harry? Well he just stood there. I wanted to know when they would be back. It was great exploring and all the people at the kennels are lovely, but they are not mum and dad!

One afternoon we had just come in from a run in the paddock and Kate was checking to make sure we had no nasty things in our coats etc. We were back in our kennel when we all heard a familiar sound. Mum's car. Even Crystal who is getting deaf looked up. Once all the gates were safely shut we charged out. It's them. What excitement! I ran round and round, and then christened one of the car wheels. Harry stood and barked, his tail wagging, and Crystal jumped up at dad. Home, we're going home. Tell you one thing. It happens every time – Crystal whines all the way home. It is getting mono.......Boring! Mum had to turn up the radio.

On the Saturday we all had a bath. Mum had told Kate that she had put smelly stuff on while she was away to prevent these things called mosquitoes from biting her. Trouble is it didn't work as she had loads of bites. Dad didn't have one! That weekend all the bites got worse, and mum had to telephone 111 service. She also had to send photos to a doctor at the hospital. First thing Monday morning she was queuing at the surgery to get antibiotics from the doctor.

You want to know about the wedding? Well, I gather it was marvellous. I heard her on the phone to her best friend. Though with having to get four trains mum said she and dad were exhausted. Yet I gather mum was so happy to see her friends again after thirteen years. They had been friends for forty-nine years. Reckon that's a long time.

Mum had taken loads of photos but didn't bore everyone with showing them all, just the main ones. Yes, before you ask, apparently her feet did hurt and she could only take small steps, from the car to the Town Hall, then the church and back to the car but the second day she wore a different dress and shoes and that was much better. We could all feel how happy mum was that she had been. It was in her voice. 'Like finding a part of me again' she said. Not quite sure what that means, except I could see she was smiling a lot when she said it, and her energy was stronger.

She told friends how helpful everyone they had met had been. Guess what? Even local police helped with their luggage when mum and dad couldn't find the right platform at a small local railway station. As to the people at the wedding, she must have liked them a lot as they were on most of the photographs, she and dad were busy showing people.

The only thing she was upset about (apart from the heat which was too much for her) was that someone stole her camera. She was telling friends that someone must have cut the cord round her wrist while she was looking in a shop. Fortunately, she took most of the photos with her camera phone, but I felt that she was sorry to have lost the camera. She said that it had been with her a long time: even longer than me. Though of course she would be dev? Well . … really upset, if she lost me, as I am irreplaceable. So now you know, I am whatever that means. Probably, that she loves me to the moon and back. She and dad love us all, but I know I am just that little bit special, though not when I play in the garden with dad's socks, and it rains! Or when I chew the wood surround which goes round the gravel.

Talking about rain, mum was so glad to come back to the cool and to find her flowers were all right. The day after we got home, we were out on the beach. I found more new friends to say hello to. It was great. Several days after that we went elsewhere, and guess what we saw?

CHAPTER NINE

Coming towards us were two Miniature Schnauzers. Both girls! They were nervous at first, but we all stopped to talk and they began to relax. That was after the initial introduction, of course. Don't think they get out much, or maybe it is that they are younger than I am. I did wonder if their mum and dad are nervous they won't come back because they did not let them off their leads, which was a shame. Funny that we always recognize others of our breed, even from a distance. What are their names? Well, I don't want to admit this, but I can't quite remember. I was too busy saying hello! It could have been something like Daisy and Willow. I'll let you know next time I see them.

Now, we come to banana skins Yes, that's right, banana skins! 'Keep the banana skins and put them in a dish with water.' This was a tip mum got from a friend of hers. Why banana skins, and what are they for? This sounds interesting. so I thought I'd sit and listen. Apparently, there is a lot of goodness in banana skins. Potassium I understand. One of mum's friends was telling her how using banana skin water and cutting up the skins and putting them near the roots of her roses would do marvels for them. Oh yeah? I shared this information with Crysal. She just sniffed, growled and turned her back on me. Honestly, some dogs are so rude. She was more interested in chewing her teeth cleaning biscuit. So, she doesn't know it all!

'It actually works' I heard mum tell dad about a week later. 'That rose has never had any buds on it whatsoever, and now look at it now. I wonder why they are not all like that?' 'It's weird' I heard her say. There was only one teensy weensy little snag with her working things out. That snag? Me! Come on now, wouldn't you investigate any new smells in your garden? The fact that there were these smelly things in flowerpots just made it more interesting. No, I didn't eat them all. I am not greedy – just curious.

Now before I go any further, I think I ought to explain, if you don't already know, I am extremely bright. I learned to speak etc at an early age. In fact, I can't remember a time when I couldn't understand. It makes everything so much easier especially when I am lying down pretending to sleep, because I can hear what mum and dad are saying.

I was out with mum on the beach the other day and I met Zeb. He is a Golden Retriever. He wasn't with his mum or his dad as they were on holiday, but I gather his mum's sister and her husband came to look after him. The first time I saw him we were both on leads and I barked at him. The second time we were on the beach, off our leads and he came over to me and we played a lovely game of chasing each other. He then dashed into the sea. I didn't follow as I do not like water.

It's bad enough that I have to stand in the bath when I am bathed. Even though I have a mat to stand on I try and get out. There is a hose in the garden, which has hot and cold water. Initially, mum used that, but she couldn't keep me still, so in the end said it was easier to put me in the bath. The only one that seems to like the hose is Crystal, but then she is funny regarding water.

CHAPTER TEN

For some reason the other day Harry would not jump up the step to come into the house, not even for food. In the end mum had to pick him up. He wouldn't bend down to eat his food either. Now that is not Harry! So, mum ended up taking him to the vet and it turns out he has, Harry that is, not the vet, arthritis in his neck and spine so it hurts him when he has to jump up. The vet gave mum some stuff for him. I heard her tell dad that she wants to find someone who does massage for animals.

She has done some herself, but she wanted someone who does it regularly. She has managed to find someone I think and will take him there soon. It is weird, cause sometimes he will jump up. Dad reckons Harry is 'putting it on'. Not sure what it means but by his voice he appears to think that Harry is kidding. Mum doesn't think so because she says that he is favouring one back leg and reckons it is worth at least one visit to have him, Harry not dad, (who I reckon is too old) checked out.

We might be going on holiday soon. I heard mum trying to arrange to rent a cottage where we can all go. Dad doesn't see why we have to go away but mum says it is a good idea to have a change of scene and all being together. 'You might as well stay at home as you'll still have to cook.' Mum said that there was a pub just down the road, so that would be fine. Not sure where we will be going except, I gather it is something to do with her book. No, I don't know what the book's about except that it's not about us. Well, mum booked this place. It is near a railway line, so might be noisy but there is loads of room for us, a whole utility room, and all fenced in outside. I think dad has had a change of heart because he asked mum if she had booked it and now seems keen to go.

Mum has been to the library to see if there is a book about this place. No, nothing, so she told dad she has ordered one from a local bookshop. They both seemed pleased as it lists circular walks. They are mum's favourite, especially if there are two versions – a long one, and a shorter one. One of the places they want to visit has a trail. Think it means a walk of some sort. It is something to do with an old story a monastery and a priest who was once a soldier..

Harry seems much better today and actually chased me round the garden. Then the gate opened, and the postman came in with a parcel. Then it was everyone for himself. I dashed over to the fence barking and looking as if I was a force to be reckoned with - that means fierce! Harry followed suit. Crystal? Well, when she actually heard we were barking she dashed outside and joined in. The postman talked to us and didn't seem at all worried. Why? 'Because he laughed and said, 'well you lot, that's a lot of noise.'

CHAPTER ELEVEN

The other afternoon Harry and I were in the kitchen. Crystal had managed to go into the lounge, and we could hear her scraping and scraping in Harry's bed trying to make it hers. I could hear mum saying 'no' to Crystal. However, she took no notice and just lay sprawled out taking up most of the room.

Apparently, Harry then wandered in. I was in the kitchen killing a rat – no not a real one – but a toy I like to shake about. It's a blue and white toy crocodile with a long tail, and I like shaking the tail. It's indestructible: that's what the blurb on the box said when mum read it out. Dad just sighed and said, 'not another toy'. Do you know at times he is a real killjoy. You just can't have too many toys especially when half of them are usually hanging on the line to dry, cause Crystal left them out in the wet. Why is it she aways takes the one I want and perhaps one of the few that hasn't been repaired time and time again.

Where was I? Oh yes, Crystal had command ...... taken Harry's bed. Mum had been reading but she had looked up and watched what was going on. Harry had walked up to the bed and looked as though he wanted to jump in. He told me later that it was his bed after all and his vetbed was in it. However, he was unsure about trying to get in with Crystal hogging all the room so hesitated and then decided better safe than sorry. Mum said that she could see him doing a lot of stretches, and yawns and walking backwards and forwards, so he was obviously not happy. He was also casting meaningful looks in Crystal's direction.

That's what I heard her say to dad. Not quite sure what she meant but I reckon Harry for once was giving Crystal the evil eye. I heard mum saying to him that she couldn't believe what she was seeing and had to try quietly to take a few photos to prove she wasn't dreaming. Dad was working on the computer in another room. Mum didn't want to break the spell so kept quiet and didn't move. What came next?

Harry was still walking up and down when I dashed into the room. It had been too quiet in the kitchen for too long, so I knew something was happening, and, of course, I didn't want to miss out. Mum said that she was watching Harry stretch out full length then walk up and down near me. We passed each other a few times and had a bit of a talk.

Crystal then decided she was bored so got out of the bed. Harry immediately went in, turned round a few times then settled down. Ok, so what I hear you say, there's nothing unusual in that. Quite right there isn't. However! By then I wanted to play more so I jumped into Harry's bed and started to play fight. Sometimes in the garden he just stands there and lets me grab one of his legs. That's no fun because he doesn't do anything. Well, to say I was surprised is an understatement. This time when I jumped into his bed and started to mouth him indicating I wanted to play he responded. He and I played together for a few minutes, then I got bored, wanted a cuddle from mum, and he curled up and dozed off.

That's when mum got up and went in to natter to dad, telling him what had happened, and that Harry and I had actually played together. 'That's nice' he said but I don't think he was really listening!

I don't know why she was making such a fuss about it as sometimes Harry and I play in the garden, and he is always barking though he always stops playing when he sees mum. No idea why – he just does. Must admit though it was the first time Harry had started a game, so maybe that's why that was special.

Crystal was padding backwards and forwards whining and looking at mum, so I reckoned it was nearly teatime, well, her teatime. Honestly, it's a wonder she is not as big as a house, as she's forever looking for food, whether it is sticking her nose into our seek and search games or trying to see if there is any remnant of food left on the plates going into the dishwasher.

Tell you what did surprise me, the other day Harry and Crystal were in the same bed, Harry's bed, in the lounge. Now, that has never happened before.

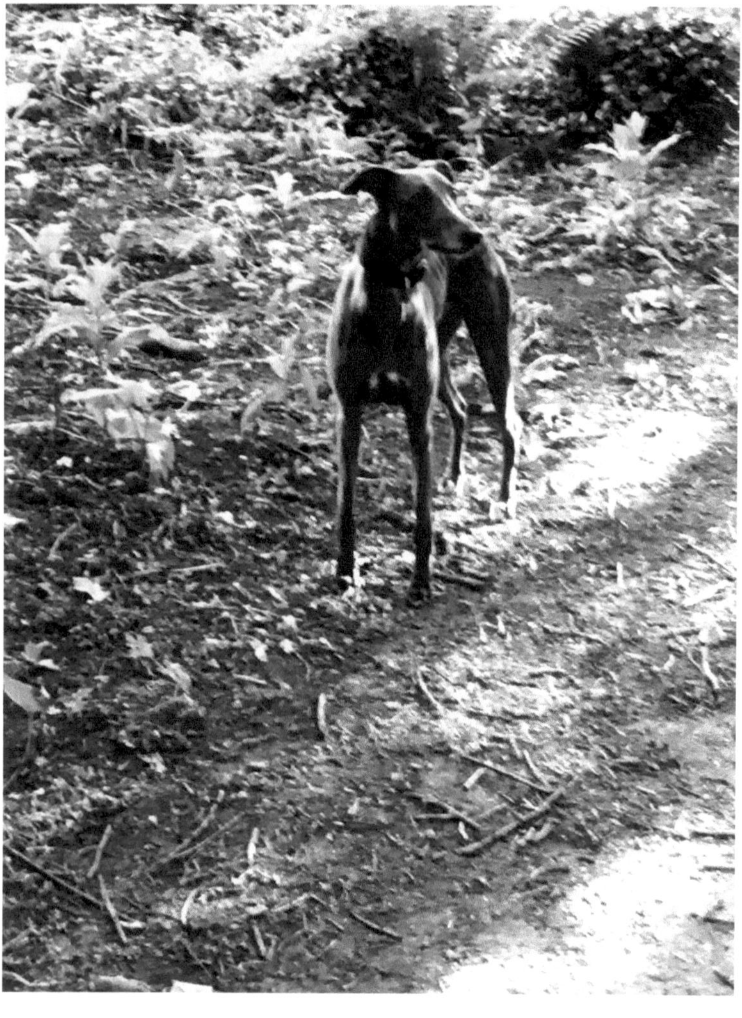

CHAPTER TWELVE

Guess what I found in the small back garden? Well, it's not a garden as such, just a small patch of grass, but mum calls it the back garden. We all had a few first in with our food. They are small and round and juicy.

When we were let out in the back garden, I could smell them and then I saw them. They were growing on bushes, and I could just about reach some of them. Blackberries! Have you had them? They are lush. That means nice. I was watching a cookery programme on the tv recently and one of the people said that she liked something called sticky toffee pudding, and that it was lush.

When she said it, she smiled so I reckoned it was a good word, and now I use it quite a lot. We just have a few blackberries as mum says not too many, but it is a change from apple. I would sneak more but mum is always there even if I hide round the corner and try and take them quietly. Unfortunately, she sees the bushes moving and knows it is me. It is a hard life!

As to other fruit, we always know when mum has an apple, not just because we see her pick one up but because we can smell it. So, if she has one, even if we have had one cut up in our food, we sit in the lounge near her feet and gaze up at her until she gives us some of hers. It is a neat trick and always works. Our eyes never leave her face. Harry has this off to a fine art. He looks so pathetic. Crystal joins in too, so you see we can share if we have to.

Tell you one funny thing about Crystal, when she is with us in the lounge waiting for apple she sits quietly, and patiently for her pieces of apple, no whining for tea.

CHAPTER THIRTEEN

Mum is making a list. No sweat, but this time we are on it. Before you ask, it isn't because we are going into kennels because they are going away again. It is because we are going with them, and mum has to make a list, so she doesn't forget any of our stuff. We are going to the place I told you about, where there is a monastery, a priest and a trail.

What sort of stuff? Well, apart from food of course, spoons, food and water bowls and our beds, things like extra towels, wet weather coats, shampoo, t r e a t s. She never goes anywhere without those. Most important.

I heard her telling a friend recently she was so embarrassed the other day. She was in a cafe getting a cup of tea and went to get the money from her coat pocket. Unfortunately, out of her pocket fell a load of poo bags. All clean of course, but the next lady in the queue bent to pick them up for her. Fortunately, that lady had dogs and like mum never went anywhere without these necessities.

I heard mum tell dad that the two of them had quite a natter about their dogs. This lady also had a rescue dog, though not like Harry. His owner had died, and the lady and her husband had taken on the elderly dog. He was a Mastiff crossed with a Rottweiler, was ten years old, and had a nasty large lump on his back leg. I heard her tell mum apparently the lump couldn't be operated on. As he was such a big dog, they had bought a car ramp. If mum had known the lady, she could have given him ours – you know the one we have never used, because ……

Anyway, from what mum was saying to dad I liked the sound of this lady because it seemed she was kind. Why do I think that? Well, she has taken on an elderly dog, who has health problems. She knows that he might only have another six months or a year to live, yet she cares enough to do everything she can. I reckon her husband must be a nice person too, don't you?

Returning to our holiday, I must tell you this. The place is called Shropshire. Mum particularly wants to go as it is something to do with a book she is writing. Dad reckoned she just needed to buy a street map, but mum says that won't do as she needs to visit the area.
As I said earlier, initially, I think dad was trying to put her off going by saying it won't be a holiday as she will still have to cook. Mum wasn't buying that because as I told you I heard her say that she would do some cooking but there was a pub down the road so they could manage for a few days. The house has a large fenced off garden, which is dog proof. So, here's hoping we all enjoy it. Also, that the weather is good. I do not like walking in the rain. Why? You know why? I do not have to spell it out for you. All I am going to say is that it involves water! Water and shampoo. Now do you understand.

CHAPTER FOURTEEN

Mum and I've been watching the television. We snuggle up together on the settee and as long as I don't dash and peer at the screen, I am ok. The other night we were watching a repeat of the Doghouse. If you haven't seen it, tune in. It is to do with finding the right dog at a particular rescue centre for all those who come to look for a new companion. Mum likes this and won't answer the 'phone when it is on.

Talking about the doghouse, I was in that myself a few days ago. Not the one on the tv, the one at our home! Apparently, these words the doghouse, mean that someone is in trouble as they have done something wrong. I did not do anything wrong. If anyone was to blame, you could say it was mum? Because she introduced us to them. Blackberries.

I've already said that at the back of the house there is a small amount of grass. In the middle is a path and there is a gate at the end. In one corner of the grass near a small wall there are things called brambles. On these brambles grow lovely, tasty things called blackberries. When they are ready to be picked these turn a lovely sort of purple colour.

We have often been in the back garden and although the brambles have always been there, we have never taken any notice of the blackberries until the day when we first had them in our food. Crystal says I should make it clear that she has never taken any notice of the blackberry bushes and in any case would not dream of helping herself. I was the one who could smell them, and I was the one who decided to help myself.

Mum was in the back garden de-heading some of the roses and we were out there with her; just mooching around, barking at anyone we could see. Suddenly I smelled something - blackberries. Naturally, I went to investigate. I spotted a bush with some low-lying branches, which just happened to be in reach of my mouth, as were the blackberries. So, I did what any self-respecting dog would do – I helped myself. Crystal and Harry could see what I was doing, but they weren't interested. Mum called but I was busy, so I ignored her; just for a few minutes – that's all it was! She came round the corner and saw me and did not seem pleased. How do I know that? Well, she spoke in a certain voice and that usually means she is not happy about something.

I did wonder that maybe if I hid in the bushes, she might not see me. However, Crystal says that she will still see them shake and will know it is me. I have asked her to give me a warning bark when she sees mum coming, but she won't do it. I reckon that is really mean! I was thinking about her the other day and thought at first that maybe she likes being mean. Of course, she is quite old now and wanders about a lot, but all she seems interested in is food and getting it before we do.

Tell you what did occur to me though. When mum takes Harry and me out, if we go anywhere near water Crystal doesn't come with us. Well, that's not strictly true; she does but only if dad is with us. We don't go in the water, but Crystal always makes a beeline for it whether it is clean or not. I am wondering if she feels a little left out of things.

CHAPTER FIFTEEN

Today it has been really hot, so mum took us out early to the park, the shady one. I've told you about that. It is the one with loads of wooden figures. Think all the visiting dogs must like those as there are loads and loads of really great smells. I left mine too. 'Olly was here' it says! Harry left his mark too.

Tomorrow Harry and mum are going to see someone who will give Harry a massage. I can't go with them if it is hot, so I hope it will be cooler. She's also heard of this place where you can take dogs to swim. It is a special pool. However, I am not sure this is a good idea because Harry is not fond of water and although he would wear a life jacket, and someone would be walking beside him in the water it might scare him. Perhaps mum will think again. I hope so.

Gosh, this is really scary. Mum has entered a competition to win a camper van. What is it? It is something like a car but bigger, and you can sleep in it. It has a space for a bed, a cooker, a shower, toilet, fridge, and table etc. I am hoping she doesn't win, because I think it will be safer if she sticks to a car. Yes, it would be lovely for us all to go on holiday together, but!

I didn't go with mum and Harry to see the McTimoney lady because it would have been too hot for me to stay in the car. Harry was very quiet when he came back and just wanted to sleep. Before he nodded off, I asked him what it was like. 'Did you enjoy it?'

He looked at me then said, 'I wasn't sure at first what was happening, but the lady was very gentle and asked mum a lot of questions.' 'And?' But he had closed his eyes and although I was frustrated, I knew he felt slightly different and needed to sleep. That evening he said that the lady had done something that felt like flicks with her fingers on various parts of his body. Later on, she used a small machine over certain areas and also used her hands to massage him. He had enjoyed it and although he was not sure what was happening, he felt it was ok, and mum was there, so he knew he was safe.

'Are you going back?' 'Think so' he yawned. 'Mum's going to get a report and will then decide'. He lay in his bed and looked at me. 'She mentioned something about a tread mill and water, but I heard mum say that she was not sure about this and would need to think.'

Harry continued. 'After the treatment mum took me to a café. I had water to drink, and she had an apple and hazelnut cake! At a table not too far away sat a man, a woman, and a Mini Schnauzer. Their dog, called Odin, was bigger than me, and a different colour. The people asked about me and the man said that he could see I was nervous. Before they left, he came over, bent down and said hello to me.'

CHAPTER SIXTEEN

I was on the beach again this morning with mum. Another early start as it was going to be hot. As we neared the steps leading to the beach a car drew up and a man got out. He opened the boot and out jumped two dogs. A Collie and a Jack Russell. The dogs dashed down the steps barking and barking and ran on the sand.

When mum let me off the lead, I thought I'd go and say hello. It was only polite as I had not seen them before. Unfortunately, the Jack Russell turned round on me, snarling, showing his teeth, and looked as though he was going to bite me. This was not good. It was scary. So, I ran back to mum who did seek and search with me until I was settled. Eventually, I saw the man and his dogs at the far end of the beach in the water. The Jack Russell was on a lead. I breathed a sigh of relief, as there were quite a few dogs about by then, and I didn't want anyone to be hurt.

However, I then met a lovely bouncy Springer Spaniel who was more than happy to play. I really enjoyed that. It was fun. Then, guess what? I saw a Mini Schnauzer in the distance. He ran towards me to say hello, then like me stopped and had a thought, then advanced.

We always recognise our own breed and today was no exception. He and I had a fantastic play. We raced round and round and round. Part way through though he came running over to mum for a treat. He must have known she always has treats, and clean poo bags in her pockets. Mum was talking to Otis's owners, but she didn't take any photos of us because she had forgotten her camera phone. Typical! I also met a Wolfhound and two Whippets. They were very laid back and happy as we all said hello and I didn't feel threatened one little bit. That was grand.

I haven't forgotten by the way about the camper van. I'm still waiting to hear if mum won it. It's quite exhausting, as every time the 'phone rings I expect to hear the worst – bad news. She's won! So, I'd really appreciate it if you sent positive thoughts for her not to win. I don't think I could stand the strain of her driving then trying to park it, especially if it is in a small space. Also, where would she park it when she's home? No news is good news they say, so fingers crossed. I'll let you know what happens. OK?

By for now. Oh, I've just remembered. I've forgotten to tell you about the stairs and the stairgate. Never mind, I'll do it next time.

Olly.

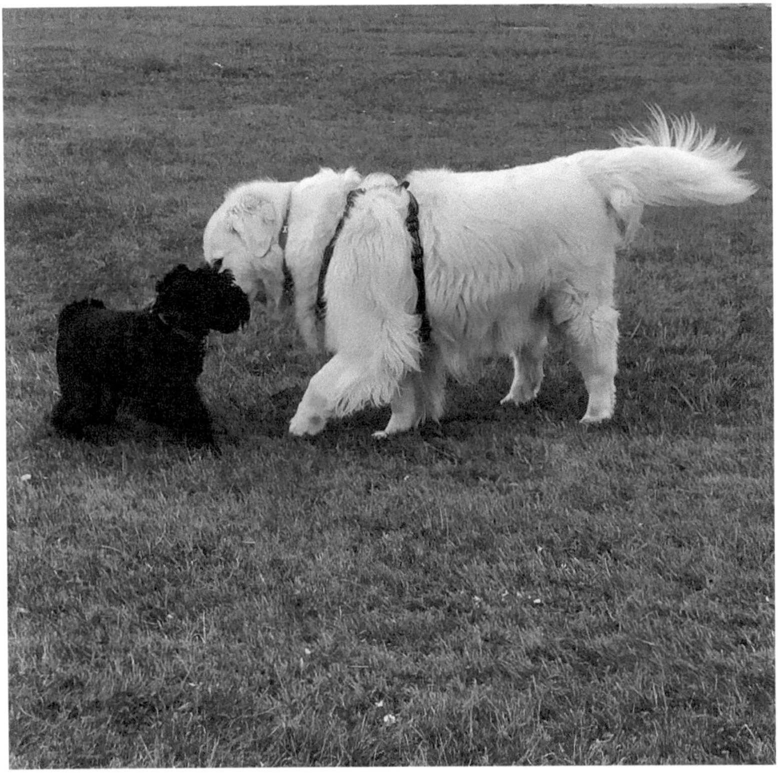

About the Author

Stefanja, who also writes as Steffi Gardner, has had dogs for well over thirty years. Most of them have been Miniature Schnauzers, though over the years two Golden Retrievers have found their way into her heart. She has been writing for almost as long, both fiction and non fiction. Her first children's book, a mix of fact and fiction is about a border collie with a difference. Charlie to the Rescue was published in November 2020. This was followed by Charlie's Quest in September 2022. She is currently working on her third children's book, and a collection of short stories, this time, for adults.

Contact the Author
e mail Steffig@gmx.com